# Sing A Song Of Ireland

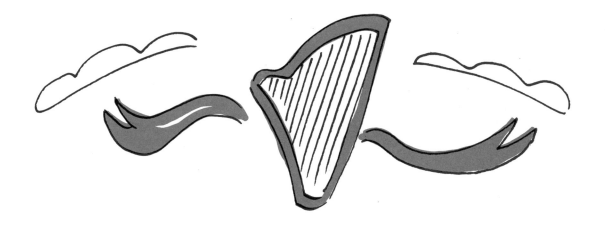

## Caroline Hooper

### Illustrated by David Meldrum

## Chester Music Limited

(A division of Music Sales Ltd.)
8/9 Frith Street, London W1V 5TZ

# Contents

Cover design by Chloë Alexander
Printed and bound in the United Kingdom by
Caligraving Limited, Thetford, Norfolk.

Order No. CH61674    ISBN 0-7119-8312-7

# The New Moon

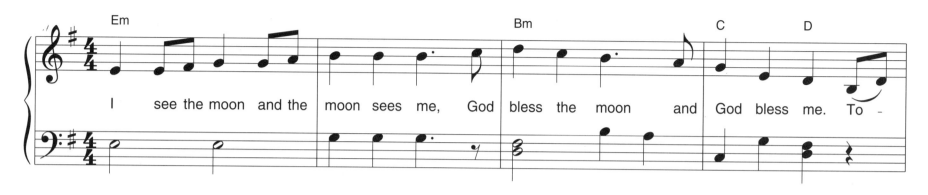

I see the moon and the moon sees me, God bless the moon and God bless me. To-

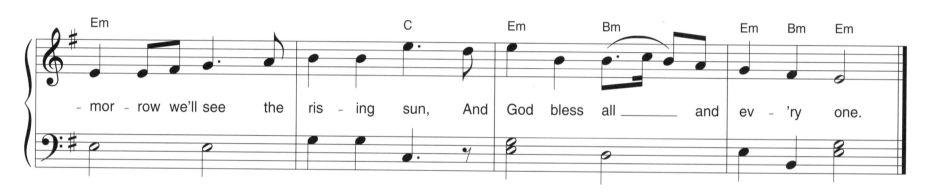

-mor - row we'll see the ris - ing sun, And God bless all _____ and ev - 'ry one.

I see the moon and the moon sees me,
God bless the moon and God bless me.
Tomorrow we'll see the rising sun,
And God bless all and ev'ry one.

This is an old Irish folk song.

# Londonderry Air

Words by W. G. Rothery

1. In Derry vale, beside the singing river,
   So oft I strayed, ah, many years ago,
   And culled at morn the golden daffodillies
   That came with Spring to set the world aglow.
   Oh, Derry vale, my thoughts are ever turning
   To your broad stream and fairy-circled lea,
   For your green isles my exiled heart is yearning,
   So far away across the sea.

2. In Derry vale, amid the Foyle's dark waters,
   The salmon leap above the surging weir.
   The sea-birds call, I still can hear them calling
   In night's long dreams of those so dear.
   Oh, tarrying years, fly faster, ever faster.
   I long to see the vale belov'd so well,
   I long to know that I am not forgotten,
   And there at home in peace do dwell.

Londonderry is a city in Northern Ireland.

Air is another word for song.

# 'Tis The Last Rose Of Summer

Words by Thomas Moore

1. 'Tis the last rose of summer left blooming alone.
All her lovely companions are faded and gone.
No flower of her kindred, no rosebud is nigh
To reflect back her blushes or give sigh for sigh.

This tune is sometimes called "The Groves of Blarney".

There is a stone at Blarney Castle in Ireland that is said to give you the 'gift of the gab' if you kiss it.

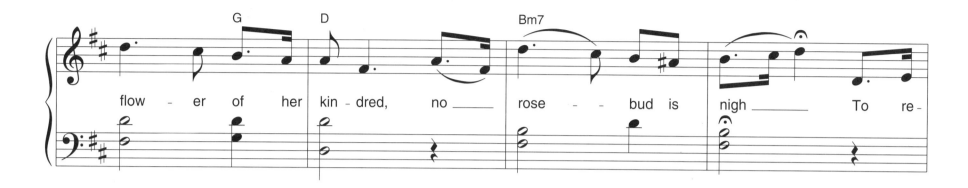

flow – er of her kin – dred, no _____ rose – – bud is nigh _____ To re-

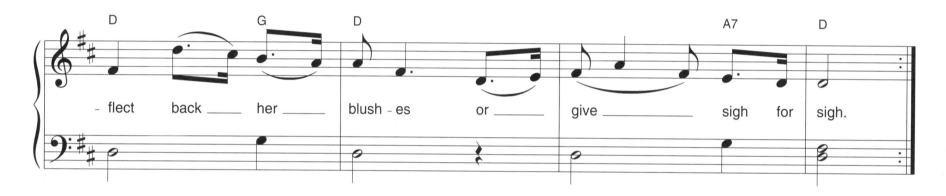

– flect back _____ her _____ blush – es or _____ give _____ sigh for sigh.

2. I'll leave thee, thou lone one to pine on a stem.
Since the lovely are sleeping, go sleep thou with them.
Thus, kindly I scatter thy leaves o'er the bed
Where thy mates of the garden lie scentless and dead.

3. So, soon may I follow, when friendships decay
And from love's shining circle the gems drop away.
When true hearts lie withered and fond ones are flown,
Oh, who would inhabit this bleak world alone?

# The Mountains Of Mourne

Words by Percy French

The people digging are actually workmen digging up a road.

Oh! Mary, this London's a wonderful sight,
Wid the people here workin' by day and by night;
They don't sow potates, nor barley, nor wheat,
But there's gangs o' them diggin' for gold in the street;

At least, when I axed them that's what I was told,
So I just took a hand at this diggin' for gold,
But for all that I found there I might as well be
Where the Mountains o' Mourne sweep down to the sea.

The man in this song has been conned into helping them for nothing.

# Believe Me, If All Those Endearing Young Charms

1. Believe me, if all those endearing young charms,
   Which I gaze on so fondly today,
   Were to change by tomorrow, and fleet in my arms,
   Like fairy gifts, fading away,
   Thou wouldst still be ador'd as this moment thou art,
   Let thy loveliness fade as it will;
   And, around the dear ruin, each wish of my heart
   Would entwine itself verdantly still!

This is a love song, so sing it quite gently and slowly.

2. It is not while beauty and youth are thine own,
   And thy cheeks unprofan'd by a tear,
   That the fervour and faith of a soul can be known,
   To which time will but make thee more dear!
   No, the heart that has truly lov'd never forgets,
   But as truly loves on to the close;
   As the sunflower turns on her god when he sets
   The same look which she turn'd when he rose.

# The Minstrel Boy

Words by Thomas Moore

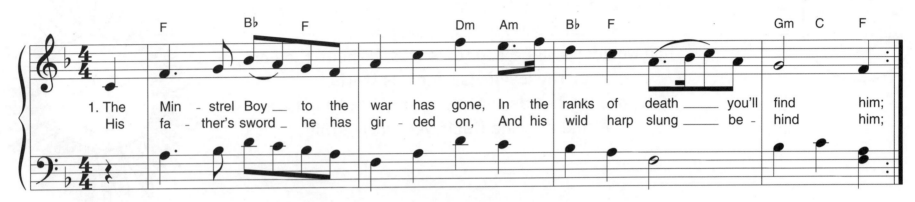

1. The Min - strel Boy __ to the war has gone, In the ranks of death _____ you'll find him;
His fa - ther's sword _ he has gir - ded on, And his wild harp slung _____ be - hind him;

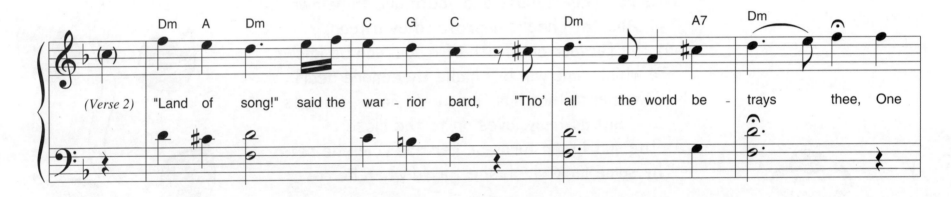

(Verse 2) "Land of song!" said the war - rior bard, "Tho' all the world be - trays thee, One

sword at least_ thy __ rights shall guard, One __ faith - ful harp_____ shall praise thee!"

1. The Minstrel Boy to the war has gone,
   In the ranks of death you'll find him;
   His father's sword he has girded on,
   And his wild harp slung behind him;
   "Land of song!" said the warrior bard,
   "Tho' all the world betrays thee,
   One sword at least thy rights shall guard,
   One faithful harp shall praise thee!"

2. The Minstrel fell! but the foeman's chain
   Could not bring that proud soul under;
   The harp he lov'd ne'er spoke again,
   For he tore its cords asunder;
   And said, "No chain shall sully thee,
   Thou soul of love and bravery!
   Thy songs were made for the pure and free,
   They shall never sound in slavery!"

# Cockles And Mussels

1. In Dublin's fair city, where girls are so pretty,
   I first set my eyes on sweet Molly Malone,
   As she wheeled her wheelbarrow through street broad and narrow,
   Crying "Cockles and mussels alive, alive o!"

   *"Alive, alive o! Alive, alive o!"*
   *Crying "Cockles and mussels alive, alive o!"*

2. She was a fishmonger, but sure 'twas no wonder,
   For so were her father and mother before;
   And they each wheeled their barrow through street broad and narrow,
   Crying "Cockles and mussels alive, alive o!"

   *"Alive, alive o...*

3. She died of a fever, and no one could save her,
   And that was the end of sweet Molly Malone;
   Her ghost wheels her barrow through street broad and narrow,
   Crying "Cockles and mussels alive, alive o!"

   *"Alive, alive o...*

Dublin is the capital city of the Republic of Ireland.

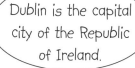
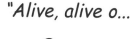

# I'll Take You Home Again, Kathleen

Words & Music by T. P. Westendorf

1. I'll take you home again, Kathleen,
Across the ocean wild and wide,
To where your heart has ever been,
Since first you were my bonnie bride.
The roses all have left your cheek,
I've watched them fade away and die;
Your voice is sad whene'er you speak,
And tears bedim your loving eyes.

Oh! I will take you back, Kathleen
To where your heart will feel no pain,
And when the fields are fresh and green,
I'll take you to your home again.

Kathleen is a popular name in Ireland.

2. I know you love me, Kathleen dear,
   Your heart was ever fond and true;
   I always feel when you are near,
   That life holds nothing, dear, but you.
   The smiles that once you gave to me,
   I scarcely ever see them now,
   Though many, many times I see,
   A dark'ning shadow on your brow.

   Oh! I will take you back, Kathleen...

# Killarney

Music by M. W. Balfe
Words by E. Falconer

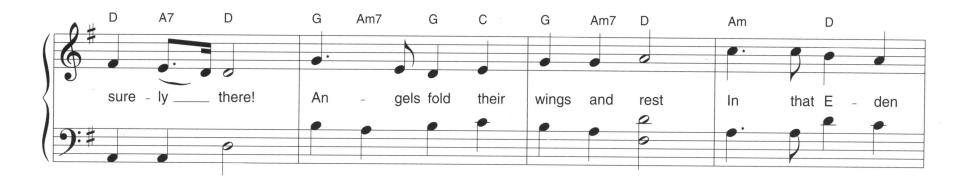

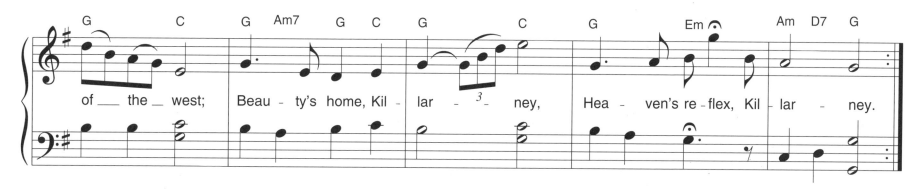

1.  By Killarney's lakes and fells,
    Em'rald Isles and winding bays,
    Mountain paths and woodland dells,
    Mem'ry ever fondly strays.
    Bounteous nature loves all lands,
    Beauty wanders ev'rywhere,
    Footprints leave on many strands,
    But her home is surely there!
    Angels fold their wings and rest
    In that Eden of the west;
    Beauty's home, Killarney,
    Heaven's reflex, Killarney.

Verdure means "fresh greenness". There is a lot of green countryside in Ireland.

2.  No place else can charm the eye
    With such bright and varied tints,
    Ev'ry rock that you pass by
    Verdure broiders or besprints.
    Virgin there the green grass grows,
    Ev'ry morn springs natal day;
    Bright hued berries daff the snows,
    Smiling Winter's frown away.
    Angels often pausing there
    Doubt if Eden were more fair;
    Beauty's home, Killarney,
    Heaven's reflex, Killarney.

# If I Get My Pick Of The Three Of Them

1. If I get my pick of the three of them,
   The three of them, the three of them,
   If I get my pick of the three of them,
   Which of them will I marry?

2. I won't marry the sailor,
   The sailor, the sailor,
   I won't marry the sailor,
   He always smells so tarry.

3. I won't marry the blacksmith,
   The blacksmith, the blacksmith,
   I won't marry the blacksmith,
   He looks so black and hairy.

4. I won't marry the tailor,
   The tailor, the tailor,
   I won't marry the tailor,
   For he might prick poor Mary!

# The Rose Of Tralee

Music by Charles W. Glover
Words by C. Mordaunt Spencer

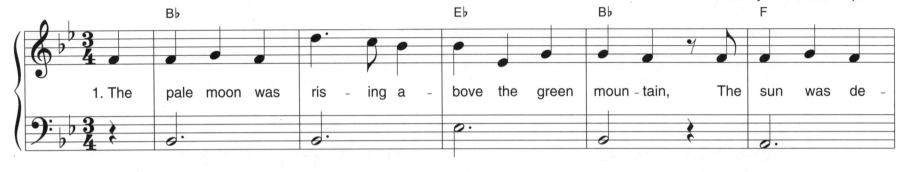

1. The pale moon was rising above the green mountain,
   The sun was declining beneath the blue sea,
When I stray'd with my love to the pure crystal fountain
   That stands in the beautiful vale of Tralee.

"Vale" is another word for valley.

23

She was lovely and fair as the rose of the summer,
Yet 'twas not her beauty alone that won me,
Oh, no! 'twas the truth in her eye ever dawning,
That made me love Mary, the Rose of Tralee.

2. The cool shades of ev'ning their mantle were spreading,
And Mary all smiling was list'ning to me,
The moon through the valley her pale rays was shedding,
When I won the heart of the Rose of Tralee.

*She was lovely and fair...*

# The Young May Moon

Words by Thomas Moore

1. The young May moon is beaming, love,
   The glow-worm's lamp is gleaming, love,
   How sweet to rove through Morna's grove,
   While the drowsy world is dreaming, love!
   Then awake! The heav'ns look bright, my dear!
   'Tis never too late for delight, my dear!
   And the best of all ways to lengthen our days
   Is to steal a few hours from the night, my dear!

2. Now all the world is sleeping, love,
   But the sage, his star-watch keeping, love,
   And I, whose star, more glorious far,
   Is the eye from that casement peeping, love!
   Then awake! Till rise of sun, my dear!
   The sage's glass we'll shun, my dear!
   For, in watching the flight of bodies of light,
   He might happen to take thee for one, my dear!

# When Irish Eyes Are Smiling

Music by Ernest Ball
Words by George Graff & Chauncey Olcott

When Irish eyes are smiling, sure it's like a morn in Spring.
In the lilt of Irish laughter, you can hear the angels sing.
When Irish hearts are happy, all the world seems bright and gay,
And when Irish eyes are smiling, sure, they steal your heart away.

# Kerry Lullaby

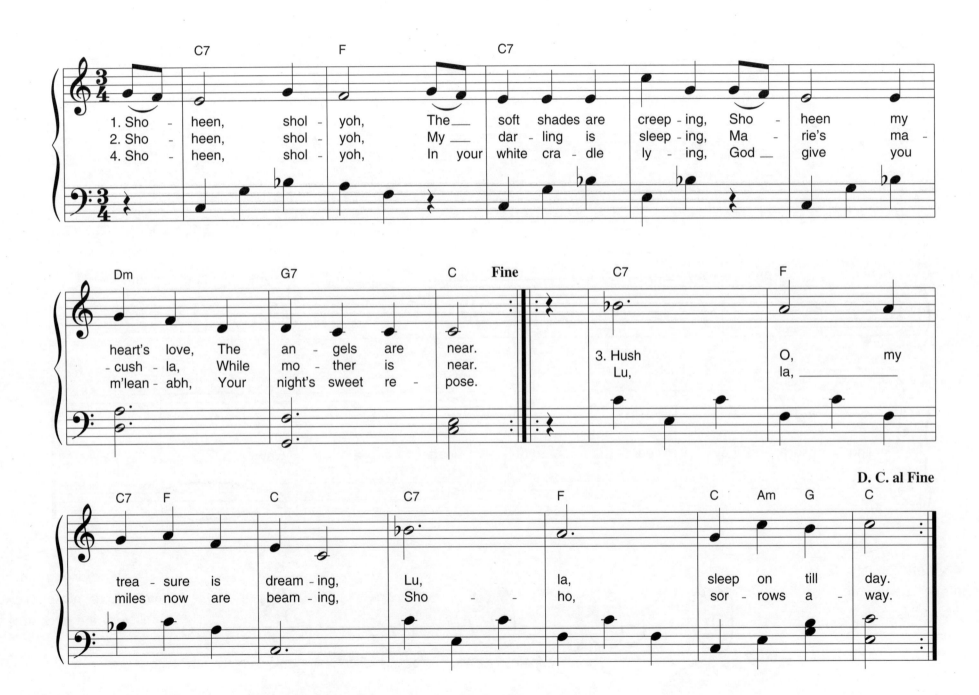

"Shoheen" and "sholyoh" are bedtime comfort words, a bit like "hush-a-bye" or "bye-byes".

Macushla means "dear", or "sweetheart".

Mo leanabh (or m'leanabh) is Irish for "my baby".

1.  Shoheen, sholyoh,
    The soft shades are creeping,
    Shoheen my heart's love,
    The angels are near.

2.  Shoheen, sholyoh,
    My darling is sleeping,
    Marie's macushla,
    While mother is near.

3.  Hush O, my treasure is dreaming,
    Lu, la, sleep on till day.
    Lu, la, miles now are beaming,
    Shoho, sorrows away.

4.  Shoheen, sholyoh,
    In your white cradle lying,
    God give you m'leanabh,
    Your night's sweet repose.

# The Harp That Once Through Tara's Halls

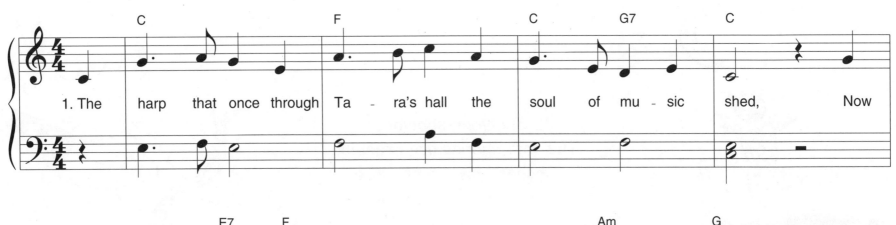

1. The harp that once through Ta - ra's hall the soul of mu - sic shed, Now

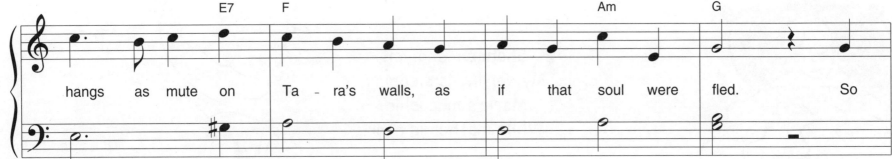

hangs as mute on Ta - ra's walls, as if that soul were fled. So

1. The harp that once through Tara's hall the soul of music shed,
Now hangs as mute on Tara's walls, as if that soul were fled.
So sleeps the pride of former days, so glory's thrill is o'er,
And hearts that once beat high for praise now feel that pulse no more.

2. No more to chiefs and ladies bright the harp of Tara's swells.
The chord alone that breaks at night its tale of ruin tells.
Thus, freedom now so seldom wakes, the only throb she gives
Is when some heart indignant breaks, to show that still she lives.

# Galway Bay

Words & Music by Arthur Colahan

there is going to be a life here-af-ter, And some-how I am sure there's going to be, I will

ask my God to let me make my hea-ven, In that dear land a-cross the I-rish sea.

1. If you ever go across the sea to Ireland,
   Then maybe at the closing of your day,
   You will sit and watch the moon rise over Claddagh,
   And see the sun go down on Galway Bay.
   Just to hear again the ripple of the trout stream,
   The women in the meadows making hay,
   And to sit beside a turf fire in the cabin,
   And watch the barefoot gossoons at their play.

2. For the breezes blowing o'er the seas from Ireland,
   Are perfumed by the heather as they blow,
   And the women in the uplands diggin' praties,
   Speak a language that the strangers do not know.
   For the strangers came and tried to teach us their way,
   They scorn'd us just for being what we are,
   But they might as well go chasing after moonbeams,
   Or light a penny candle from a star.

3. And if there is going to be a life hereafter,
   And somehow I am sure there's going to be,
   I will ask my God to let me make my heaven,
   In that dear land across the Irish sea.

Gossoon means "boy".
It usually refers to a
servant-boy.

# That's An Irish Lullaby

Words & Music by J. R. Shannon

1. Over in Killarney,
Many years ago,
Me mither sang a song to me
In tones so sweet and low,
Just a simple little ditty,
In her good ould Irish way,
And I'd give the world if she could sing
That song to me this day.

"Toora loora looral,
Toora loora li,
Toora loora looral,
Hush now, don't you cry!
Toora loora looral,
Toora loora li,
Toora loora looral,
That's an Irish lullaby."

A ditty is a simple little song.

2. Oft in dreams, I wander
To that cot again,
I feel her arms a-huggin' me
As when she held me then,
And I hear her voice a-hummin'
To me as in days of yore,
When she used to rock me fast asleep
Outside the cabin door.

*"Toora loora looral...*

# Danny Boy

Words by Frederick Edward Weatherly

1. Oh, Danny Boy, the pipes, the pipes are calling,
   From glen to glen, and down the mountain side,
   The summer's gone, and all the roses falling,
   It's you, it's you must go and I must bide.
   But come ye back when summer's in the meadow,
   Or when the valley's hush'd and white with snow.
   'Tis I'll be there in sunshine or in shadow,
   Oh, Danny Boy, oh Danny Boy, I love you so!

2. But if ye come, when all the flow'rs are dying,
   And I am dead, as dead I well may be,
   Ye'll come and find the place where I am lying,
   And kneel and say an *Ave* there for me;
   And I shall hear, tho' soft your tread above me,
   And all my dreams will warm and sweeter be.
   If you won't fail to tell me that you love me,
   Then I shall sleep in peace until you come to me!

# My Love's An Arbutus

1. My love's an arbutus
   By the borders of Lene,
   So slender and shapely
   In her girdle of green;
   And I measure the pleasure
   Of her eyes' sapphire sheen,
   By the blue skies that sparkle
   Through that soft branching screen.

2. But though ruddy the berry
   And snowy the flower,
   That brighten together
   The arbutus bower,
   Perfuming and blooming
   Through sunshine and shower,
   Give me her bright lips
   And her laugh's pearly dower.

3. Alas, fruit and blossom
   Shall lie dead on the lea,
   And Time's jealous fingers
   Dim your young charms, Machree.
   But unranging, unchanging
   You'll still cling to me
   Like the evergreen leaf
   To the arbutus tree.

# The Garden Where The Praties Grow

Words & Music by Johnny Patterson

1. Have you ever been in love my boys or have you felt the pain?
I'd sooner be in jail myself than be in love again.
For the girl I loved was beautiful I'd have you all to know,
And I met her in the garden where the praties grow.

She was just the sort of creature boys that Nature did intend
To walk right through the world my boys without the Grecian bend,
Nor did she wear a chignon, I'd have you all to know,
And I met her in the garden where the praties grow.

Praties are potatoes.

A long time ago, people who stooped forward when they walked were said to have the "Grecian bend".

2. Says I "My pretty Kathleen, I'm tired of single life,
And if you've no objection, sure, I'll make you my sweet wife,"
She answered me right modestly and curtsied very low,
"O you're welcome to the garden where the praties grow."

She was just the sort of creature...

# The Gentle Maiden

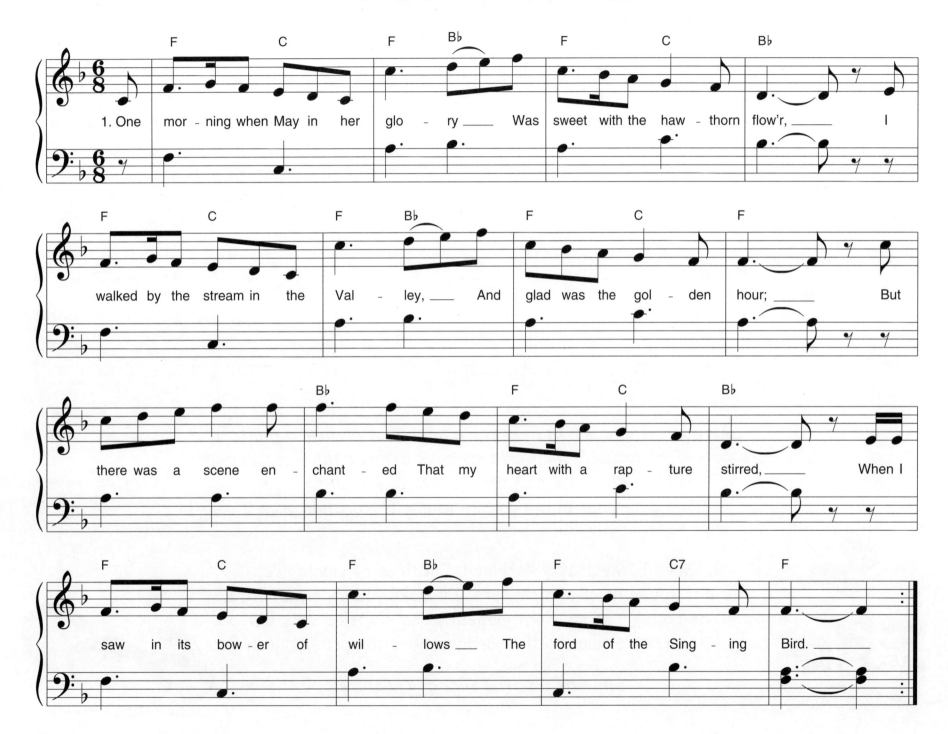

1.  One morning when May in her glory
    Was sweet with the hawthorn flow'r,
    I walked by the stream in the Valley,
    And glad was the golden hour;
    But there was a scene enchanted
    That my heart with a rapture stirred,
    When I saw in its bower of willows
    The ford of the Singing Bird.

2.  And over the white stone a-stepping
    A girl with a cloak of red,
    Came smiling a happy good morning,
    I think 'twas good morn she said,
    O I wish I had chanced to speak then,
    But I managed not e'er a word;
    Just stood and gazed after the colleen
    By the ford of the Singing Bird.

# Gaelic Cradle Song

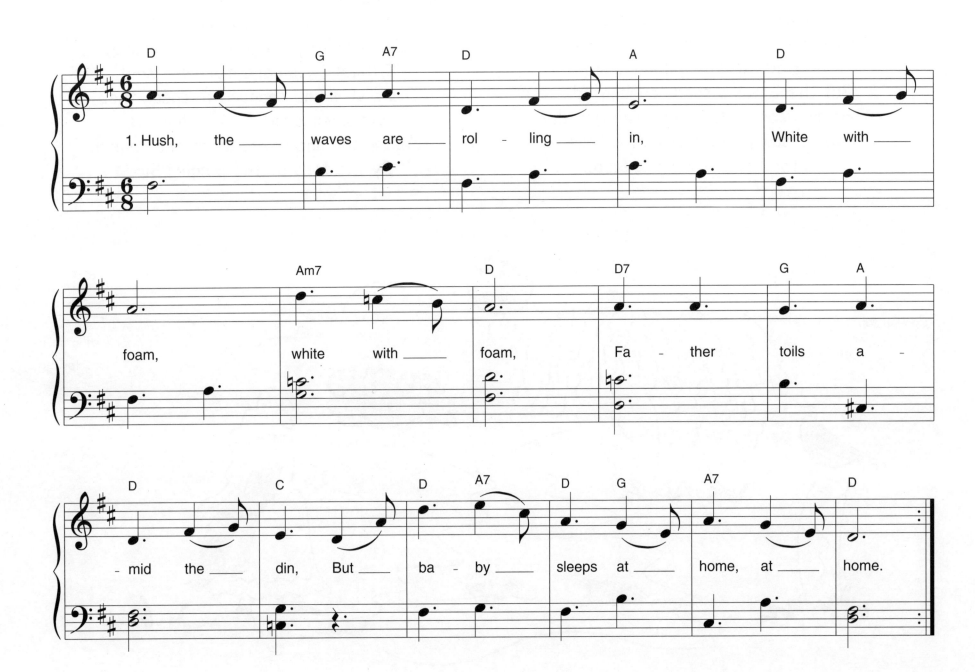

1. Hush, the waves are rolling in,
   White with foam, white with foam,
   Father toils amid the din,
   But baby sleeps at home, at home.

2. Hush, the winds roar hoarse and deep,
   On they come, on they come,
   Brother seeks the lazy sheep,
   But baby sleeps at home, at home.

3. Hush, the rain sweeps o'er the knowes,
   Where they roam, where they roam,
   Sister goes to seek the cows,
   But baby sleeps at home, at home.

# The Meeting Of The Waters

Words by Thomas Moore

1. There is not in the wide world a valley so sweet
As that vale in whose bosom the bright waters meet,
   Oh! The last rays of feeling and life must depart,
Ere the bloom of that valley shall fade from my heart.

Repeat the last line of each verse.

2. Yet it was not that Nature had shed o'er the scene
   Her purest of crystal and brightest of green;
   'Twas not her soft magic of streamlet or rill,
   Oh! No, it was something more exquisite still.

3. 'Twas that friends, the belov'd of my bosom, were near
   Who made ev'ry dear scene of enchantment more dear,
   And who felt how the best charms of Nature improve,
   When we see them reflected from looks that we love.

4. Sweet vale of Avoca how calm could I rest
In thy bosom of shade, with the friends I love best,
Where the storms that we feel in this cold world should cease,
And our hearts, like thy waters, be mingled in peace.

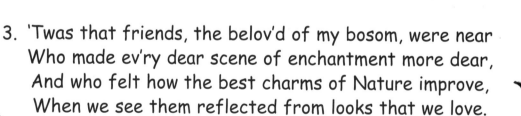

# Golden Cradle

The words in the last line are just comfort words.

Sweet babe, a golden cradle holds thee,
Soft snow white fleece enfolds thee,
Fairest flow'rs are strewn before thee,
Sweet birds warble o'er thee.
Shoheen sholo! Lu, lu, lo, lo!